# Diary of a Farmer

## Angela Royston

Raintree

Raintree is an imprint of Capstone Global Library Limited, a company incorporated in England and Wales having its registered office at 7 Pilgrim Street, London, EC4V 6LB – Registered company number: 6695582

To contact Raintree:
Phone: 0845 6044371
Fax: + 44 (0) 1865 312263
Email: myorders@raintreepublishers.co.uk
Outside the UK please telephone +44 1865 312262

Text © Capstone Global Library Limited 2014
First published in hardback in 2014
The moral rights of the proprietor have been asserted.

Edited by Daniel Nunn, Rebecca Rissman, and Catherine Veitch
Designed by Cynthia Della-Rovere
Picture research by Ruth Blair
Production by Victoria Fitzgerald
Originated by Capstone Global Library Ltd
Printed and bound in China by South China Printing Company Ltd

ISBN 978 1 406 26066 3
17 16 15 14 13
10 9 8 7 6 5 4 3 2 1

**British Library Cataloguing in Publication Data**
Royston, Angela.
Diary of a farmer.
630-dc23
A full catalogue record for this book is available from the British Library.

**Acknowledgements**
We would like to thank the following for permission to reproduce photographs: Corbis pp. 10, 21 (© Monty Rakusen/cultura), 18 (© Kathy Coatney/AgStock Images), 24 (© Helen King); Getty Images pp. 6 (Chris Ratcliffe/Bloomberg), 16 (Digital Vision), 17 (Visuals Unlimited, Inc./Nigel Cattlin), 19 (Michael Blann), 20 (Georgia Glynn Smith), 23 (Tim Graham), 25 (Rick Gerharter); Shutterstock pp. contents page, 15 (© Richard Thornton), title page, 12 (© Bas Meelker), 4 (© Khvost), 5 (© basketman23), 9 (© Pixel 4 Images), 13 (© Andrew Roland), 22 (© auremar), 28 pen (© Ingvar Bjork), 28 diary (© sauletas); Superstock pp. 7 (Vandersar, Terry J.D.), 8 (Gari Williams / age footstock), 11 (Imageshop), 14 (Design Pics), 26 (The Irish Image Collection), 27 (Prisma).

Background and design features reproduced with permission of Shutterstock. Cover photograph of farmer in field reproduced with permission of Corbis (© Juice Images).

We would like to thank Paul Miller for his invaluable help in the preparation of this book.

Every effort has been made to contact copyright holders of material reproduced in this book. Any omissions will be rectified in subsequent printings if notice is given to the publisher.

All the Internet addresses (URLs) given in this book were valid at the time of going to press. However, due to the dynamic nature of the Internet, some addresses may have changed, or sites may have changed or ceased to exist since publication. While the author and publisher regret any inconvenience this may cause readers, no responsibility for any such changes can be accepted by either the author or the publisher.

Some words are shown in bold, **like this**. You can find out what they mean by looking in the Glossary.

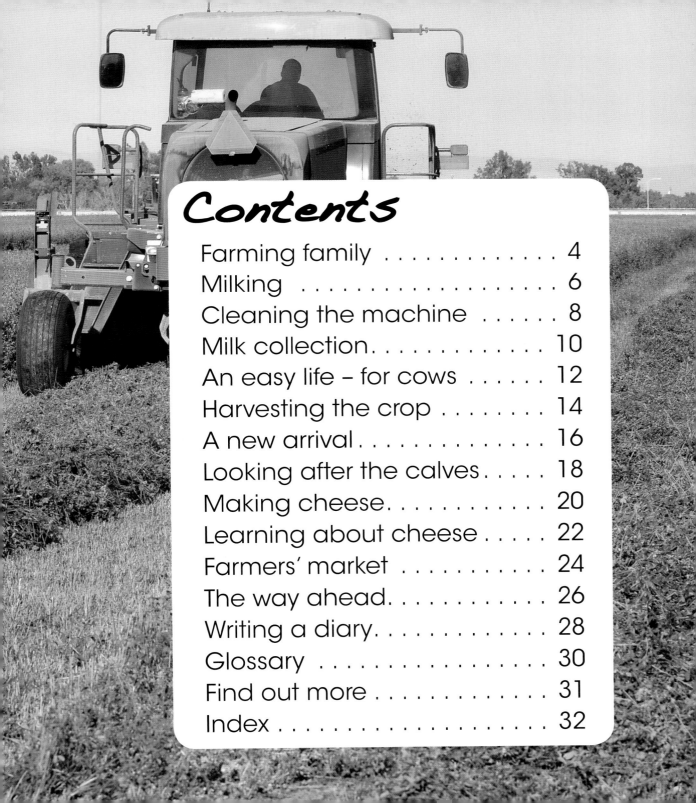

# Contents

# Farming family

I am a farmer and my parents are farmers. My great-grandparents started this **dairy farm** nearly 100 years ago. We have 130 cows that we milk twice a day.

These cows produce a lot of milk. That is why we farm them!

My grandparents wouldn't recognize the farm today. We have five times as many cows as they did, and we use modern machines. We still work hard though, as this diary will show!

5

# Milking

## Monday 5 April

As usual, I was up early today. I herded the cows into the **milking parlour** to be hooked up to the milking machines. Dad helped me.

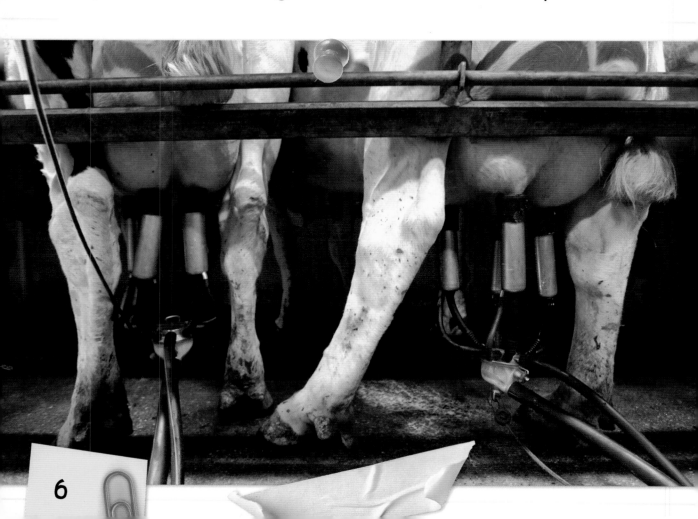

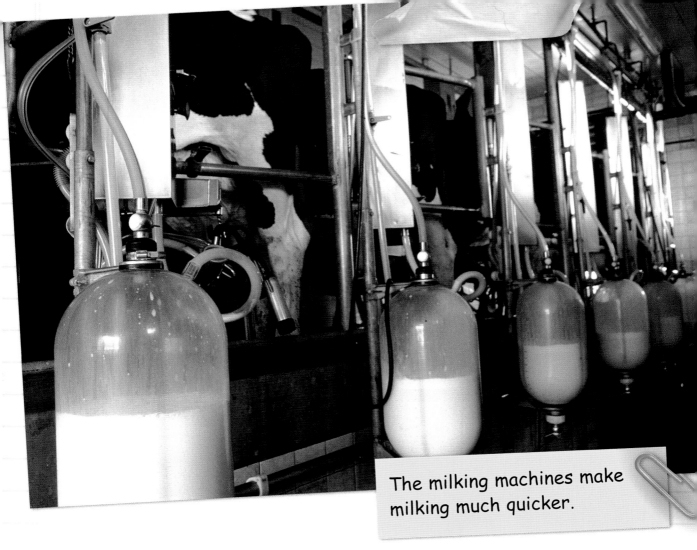

The milking machines make milking much quicker.

A milking machine is gentle, and very **hygienic**. We cleaned each cow's **teats** before we attached her to the machine. The milk was then pumped along pipes into huge containers.

# Cleaning the machine

When the milking was finished, we cleaned each cow's **teats** again and washed the floor. The milking machines were thoroughly cleaned, too.

We sometimes shower the cows too!

By the end of the day, I'm too tired to move!

It is very important to keep the **milking parlour** and the equipment completely clean all the time. We repeated the whole process when we milked all the cows again this evening.

# Milk collection

## Tuesday 6 April

The tanker comes every day to collect the milk from our containers. The driver empties the containers and we check the amount. Today the tanker was very late.

The driver was grumpy when he got here. He said he was late because he was held up in the traffic. He lost no time in attaching the pipe from the container to the tanker.

# An easy life - for cows

After the tanker drove away, I went down to the big field to check the cows. They were happy, munching grass in the sunshine. Lucky them!

trough

Then I checked the cows' shed to make sure it was clean. I filled up their water and food **troughs**. The shed is open on one side so the cows can wander in and out.

13

# Harvesting the crop

## Wednesday 7 April

After the sunny weather we've had recently, the grass is ready for cutting to make **silage**. Silage contains grass and other plants and makes great food for cows.

I got the tractor out, and hitched up the mower. As I drove the tractor up and down the field, the mower cut the grass and arranged it in rows.

# A new arrival

## Thursday 8 April

A cow called Clara gave birth to a calf today. The birth went well and we called the calf Dora. As soon as she was born, we tagged her ear.

Each calf is tagged so that we know for sure which calf is which!

tag

Clara licked Dora dry and then we took Dora away and milked Clara. Clara mooed for Dora for a few hours, but then forgot about her.

# Looking after the calves

We took Dora to the calf shed to join the other newborn cows. We gave her Clara's first milk to drink because it is full of **nutrients**.

Dora was already able to stand on her wobbly legs. We have 50 more cows that will give birth during the next few months. We're going to be very busy!

# Making cheese

## Friday 9 April

We keep some of our milk to make cheese. Today some school children visited the **dairy** to watch how we do it. First, the children saw the tank where the milk is separated into solid **curds** and liquid **whey**.

curds

They thought the curds smelled disgusting, and quickly moved on to the next stage! However, they loved the taste of the finished cheese.

# Learning about cheese

The **dairy** was my idea and I'm very proud of it. I told the children how I set it up with Tara, a friend I met at **agricultural college**.

This is Tara at agricultural college.

Tara and I make many traditional cheeses.

I was keen to make cheese on the farm. We get paid very little for each litre of milk – much less than the shop price. We can charge more for our **traditional** cheeses.

# Farmers' market

## Saturday 10 April

This morning I got up even earlier than usual so I could set up our stall at the local **farmers' market**. Tara and I take it in turns to sell our cheese there.

This stall sells a lot of fresh vegetables.

There was another stall selling cheese at the market today. Our regular customers know me well, though. They still bought lots of our cheese!

# The way ahead

## Sunday 11 April

While I milked the cows this morning, I started to think about the future. We could buy more cows and employ someone to help us look after them.

I'd like to sell more fancy cheese like these.

I'd like to expand the **dairy** too, and sell different cheeses. I'd also like to sell more cheese through our website on the internet.

# Writing a diary

You can write a diary too! Your diary can describe your life – what you saw, what you felt, and the events that happened. Writing a diary is a great way to help us remember the things that happened in our lives.

Diaries can be important. We have learned a lot from the diaries of people who lived in the past. Samuel Pepys wrote a famous diary about the Great Fire of London in 1666.

Here are some tips for writing a diary:

- Start each entry with the day and the date. You don't have to include an entry for every day.

- The entries should be in **chronological** order, which means that they follow the order in which events happened.

- Use the past tense when you are writing about something that has already happened.

- Remember that a diary is the writer's story, so use "I" and "my".

# Glossary

**agricultural college** place where people study different types of farming

**chronological** in order of time

**curds** solids made when the fatty parts of milk stick together

**dairy** place where milk is made into cheese, cream, butter, or other milk products

**dairy farm** a farm that keeps cows or goats so that their milk can be collected and sold

**farmers' market** market with stalls where farmers sell fresh food which has been grown or made on their own farms

**hygienic** clean and free from germs

**milking parlour** large shed where machinery for milking cows or goats is kept

**nutrients** parts of food that a living thing needs to be healthy

**silage** grass and other plant matter that is collected and stored as food for cattle

**teat** part of a cow where milk leaves her body

**traditional** ways of doing things that have been followed for many years

**trough** long narrow container that holds food or water for animals

**whey** liquid left behind when curds are removed from milk

# Find out more

## Books

*Clarabelle: Making Milk and So Much More*, Cris Peterson (Boyds Mills Press, 2007)

*Jobs on a Farm* (World of Farming), Nancy Dickmann (Raintree, 2010)

*Let's Visit a Dairy Farm*, Alyse Sweeney (Children's Press (CT), 2006)

*What Happens at a Dairy Farm?* (Where People Work), Kathleen Pohl (Weekly Reader Early Learning, 2006)

## Websites

**www.agclassroom.org/kids/tours.htm**
On this website you can find out about a farming family, the life of a cow, and much more.

**www.dairyfarmingtoday.org/Learn-More/faq/Pages/AboutCows.aspx**
This website will give you some facts and figures about how much milk cows produce each day, and how much they eat. Click on "Life on the Farm" to learn about a farming family. The site includes a dictionary, too.

**www.kidsfarm.com/**
Visit this website for information about all types of farm animals, and lots more. Click on "Equipment" and then on "Cut" to find out more about the machines that cut crops.

# Index